PLETHORA OF INKED EMOTIONS

A COMPILATION OF ALL MY POEMS.

BELINDA LAVENDER

Copyright © Belinda Lavender
All Rights Reserved.

To all those who love,

To all those who hate

To all those with heart break; And

To all those who are out there struggling.

Contents

Contents

Foreword

These poems are a sensitive girl's response to her own inner turmoil as well as to the ills she finds around. Loneliness, feelings of guilt at causing hurt to others & the longing for love are compensated somewhat by the exhilaration of the poetic impulse, the joy of expressing herself and the release that comes through it. Belinda Lavender is seized of the fundamental facts of the female body. It bleeds & you are caught up in all the taboos & rituals. It attracts the wrong responses. Age is no protection against the male gaze and the male hands. The relationship is of predator & prey, not of the rainbow romance between lover & beloved.

And then there are the inequalities & discriminations against the low caste, the dark skinned, the poor.

Belinda Lavender has a sense of rhyme & rhythm. Her language holds promise.

Prof. Lakshmi M. Padmanabhan,
MA. Eng Lang & Lit
(Producer of Kambhoji film,
Free lancer & Vlogger @ Gandhigiri)

Acknowledgements

I pay my sincere gratitude to all those who supported me, letting me analyse and upbring my writing.

Publishing a book is harder than I thought and more rewarding than I could have ever imagined. None of this would have been possible without my best friends, who lend all their time to read, correct, encourage and appreciate my writings. They stood by me during every struggle and all my successes. That is true friendship.

I'm eternally grateful to my sister Tushaara, who took in an extra mouth to feed when she didn't have to. She taught me discipline, tough love, manners, respect, and so much more that has helped me succeed in life. I truly have no idea where I'd be if she hadn't become another mother and a best friend to figure what I desperately needed at that age.

Thank you for all the special people who played a very important in my life.

Writing a book about the story of your life in bits as poetries is a surreal process. I'm forever indebted to Sivarama Krishnan for his editorial help, keen insight, and ongoing support in bringing my poems to life. It is because of his efforts and encouragement that I have a talent to showcase to the world.

To my family. To Amma: for always being the person I could turn to during those dark and desperate years. She sustained me in ways that I never knew that I needed.

To Pappa: for always taunting me and making me want to write more.

To my Sister, Tushaara: It is that I am so thankful to just have you in

ACKNOWLEDGEMENTS

my life.

To Achamma: for always supporting me no matter how hard or harsh I had been to you.

To Aaya: For having immense belief in me and for her continuos encouragement.

Thank you to all those who have been a part of my getting there: Naveena Vaishnavi, Akshayaa, Rishivandya, Sivarama Krishnan, Gokul Aditya, Both the Keerthanas, Ajanya and many more who encouraged me and helped me recognize what talents I had.

Thank you to all the people who had given me heartbreaks, with and without intentions; If not for you I'd not have known what writing was to me.

Finally, To the most beautiful teachers of my life: Mrs. R Shanthi and Mrs. G. Mallika, who always expected a little more than I was and wanted me to reach heights.

Author

Instagram handle: @belinda_lavender

A poetic mind with a handful of knowledge, born in 'the little England' of India. Belinda believes in fate and love more than any possible thing in the world. She always surrounds herself around the positive vibes. But she faced a lot of struggles just as from the early age of adolescence which is one of the reason she started writing. Her family showed her how not to love and be loved. Her works have all kinds of emotions a person could go through. Her rage towards the oppression over women was the key to her start of this journey. She believes in the quote, "Age is just a number" and wants people to achieve no matter how old they are.

Belinda is a budding writing, who's experience is less than what you feel in reading her works. She has proven that, a little knowledge of words and a plethora of emotions can make you do what you love. And also want people to know that, love is the only force that is capable of transforming anything.

1. A Dagger of thoughts

It struck me hard every night,
For I was an unloved child,
Sleepless nights and endless pain,
For it was a scar in my heart,
Wounded with words, deeply I was
Away from the world, away from myself
Weeping alongside blackness,
The cold breeze accompanied hushing,
Ink and paper my only companions,
Not to overlook the lonesome thoughts,
As the tear droplets fell on the sheets,
Emotions flowed as verses,
A little maiden carved herself,
From the rock people had made her.
It was traumatizing, the past
Little of memory recalled the heartache
Pages overflowed with words of grief
Losing myself for nonentity of happiness
Hoping for betterment, hoping for love,
I died around a million deaths,
My hopes were broken down,
Each time I wanted to fly,

My voice were trampled down,
And all I could do was cry,
It took me infinity
To weep and to whine,
To wail and to wear-out
And To combat and carve out my life.

2. A lesson for life

I fell for few they were all a lesson for life
I fell for one he was, life
It feels like I am not worth
But, he lets me know I am worth
It feels like I can never be me
But, he proved me wrong
It is him I want to be
But, I don't know if this will last
It was me who desired a true one
But, does love suit me?
It was he who approached me
But, can I be the one he loves?
I fell for few they were all a lesson for life
I fell for one he was, life
It made my legs shiver
But, he stood beside me
It felt like I would miserably fall
But, when I was beside him I never feared
It brought me down each time I think about future
But, he from afar held my hands and assured
It felt like heaven
But, will it last?

It felt like a last-life togetherness
But, what if it was just an illusion?
I fell for few they were all a lesson for life
I fell for one he was, life
It feels like I had chosen the right person
But, I have lost belief in myself
It is love that had made me like this
But, will love stay with me?
It is me who would go to any extent for him
But, what if we don't get together?
It was never easy to be one who people need
But, will people understand me?
It is a relation to be lasted
But, will the lesson I learnt be made to learn again?

3. A poetry she was

She was gleeful,
She was despondent,
She was she,
A poetry, so beautiful.

Some let down tears,
knowing her misery,
Some grinned like a Cheshire cat,
feeling her merriment.

She was of mixed emotions,
Sometimes too wordy,
Sometimes curt and concise,
An angelic, godlike poetry .

Air filled with perpetual laughter,
Surrounding so dull and gloomy, in
world changed as her words did,
A poetry, half or never read.

Life was a whirlwind,
enjoyable sometimes,

Formidable sometimes,
A poetry of different forms.

People admired and dismired,
People liked and disliked,
I was one's perspective,
A poetry with different meanings.

A poetry she was,
A beautiful one,
Sad, happy or any emotion,
A poetry one must read.

4. A Tale of Honesty and Betrayal

Once there lived two people
Honesty and Betrayal
Honesty loved betrayal
and Betrayal betrayed
She spent lonely nights
Weeping on her pillow
And falling into depression
It took a while for her to
Come out of her insecurity
And, she did win over it
Once she did. and then
Betrayal betrayed in the name of honesty
She was very much sure on
Not going back to him
But she did love him truely
And she wanted to give him a chance
But as she expected,
he had never changed
and had the same motive,
To betray Honesty

And the tale represented the
Repeated love life of human race
and that was the tale of honesty and betrayal.

5. A Void Within

I feel weak, miserably weak,
That my legs trembled like I'd fall,
That all the happiness around me,
Are just momentary,
That all the pain I feel,
Is something no one could ever heal.
My heart's at misery,
It aches to pull myself back,
To think everything's alright,
To hope for nothing but good.
Hurting a very close peer, unintentionally.
I felt a thousand stabbing knives,
In and out of the little heart,
The tears I witnessed,
It broke me into smithereens,
A friendship and love, broken
The root of it being me.
For the first time ever in life
I felt pain for someone else's hurt
"Why did you have to?" his eyes spoke
I did, justifying my stand, a cowardly act.
Like the sky and the stars, always together,

I want my stars to choose me,
Over anything and everything.
Little did I hurt everyone around,
Intentionally or unintentionally.
Apologize, is all I could do
But, it can't mend a broken heart, can it?
I was rude and arrogant,
And also aggressive, people called me
Little did they know, it was all masked.
Smile over frown, anguish over hurt,
That's how it was, my feelings – curt
A void within, like an incomplete poem
Emotions lacking, like an alexithymic.

6. Aeon of isolation

Short were days and long were nights,
Away from people, and my mom was right,
Fun was aside, cause' fear stood upright,
Not about myself but about the plight,
For life, I saw young people fight,
And for a year and so, nothing was alright,
As days passed schedules became tight,
For we worked till midnight,
Everything was different yesternight,
Will it be the same in fortnight?
Nights were black and days were white,
It took days for us to see the light,
Hope wasn't 'will' but just a 'might',
Will it be okay overnight?
Being far, I had a fright,
If staying away from them was right,
I saw a fighting knight,
The one working all night,
To make sure everything is alright,
And shoo away the monstrous plight,
Thinking all night, for I was fright,
This, I write, under the moonlight.

7. And then there were none

I stood alas without any more hope,
I craved for more love
I always needed people around me
I was stupid to long for temporary things
Then there I stood hopeless
I was never a one being loved
I was never a one being needed
I was always a problem
I was always a contumacious
Then there was me, drowning into blues
Wanting more of care and compassion
Wanting to want people to want me
Wanting a shoulder to lean on to
Wanting to never lose my special ones
Then I thought I got treasures
Wanting of a reason to smile
Wanting a reason to pull myself out of the gloom
Wanting to no more crave for attention
Wanting to be myself again
Then there were people who stood by my side

Holding my hands, wanting me to reach heights
I was myself again
I wanted to hold onto my people
I wanted to let myself melt in their lives
I wanted to be the 'one' for them
And then there were none.

8. As of it was a dream

Demise was just a word,
Until I experienced it through you.
You were my world,
And now we ain't together.
You, were always around me,
when nobody did.
But now my heart aches,
Thinking I couln't be there for you.
When I was with you,
I always felt love.
And, now I am much agitated,
For you left me all alone,
As if it was a dream.
Being with you, taught me many,
Most of all what I leart was;
Love is a language,
That never need another to express.

9. Bipolarity

Bipolarity of my head,
Self-centered and self-doubted
Either of it is always an extreme
For once it says —
"Life is hard only on me,
Ups and downs all in a flash
No friends to believe
No one to trust
No one to show
My weaker self"
It starts with a little hesitation,
The end always a destructed heart,
And mourning over the already dead past.
And for once it says —
"Life is easy and I am too lucky,
It feels like I'm on the top of the world,
There isn't one like me,
The isn't one superior to me
There isn't a thing I feel weak about."
It starts off with a little confidence
But instead ends off with little arrogance
And a lot of egotism.

It is me, the same me,
Who is way too beautiful at times,
And way too ugly too
Who is very much gossipy,
And very tongue-tied too
Who is the same me
But of bipolarity.

10. Bitch

Sometimes I feel,
I was never cared,
I was never loved,
I was never in any of my people's mind.
I fight for survival,
And all I get is a name BITCH
Should I not be myself?
Is it a sin or what?
Sometimes I fall so deeply,
That I do everything they would ask for,
If once I deny,
I, stamped as a BITCH again.
I hear a lot of people gossiping about,
My attitude, my height,
My language, my parents,
On the whole, ME.
Am I that bad?
Am I not worth being loved?
Should I not be myself?
Can't I fight for my survival?
I am bit a bitch,
I am just a growing girl.

Fighting for my survival,
who'se being called a bitch.

11. Caged Conquerors

Inked my emotions into the world of pages,
My voice, silenced over societal regimes.
Nights choked me till my breath was out,
Sobs were called an attention grabber.
Casteism, racism, and religious discrimination,
World is of blood sheds far and wide,
Life is miserably for the so called lowly lives,
Being stamped on for years, over the same old wound.
The prejudistic's hatred burning inside and out
Populaces being tyrannized and curbed
Depriving from one's customs and culture
Suppressing for the identity one owns,
And the attire one wears and the language one speaks,
And the every other difference one can ever have.
One being called filthy, because he's of low caste
Another being called a whore, because she's lowly
One being called a rapist, because he's of dark race
Another being called a bawd, just because-
Because she doesn't fall under the socially set boundaries.
World doesn't go easy on these people,
People who suffer for the things that's not theirs to own,
Atheists and agnostics, roused from all the religions,

Because there was no hope to crawl on to,
Because there was no way out of all their sufferings,
Because there was no solution to their problems.
Trapped into the stares of the preying eyes
Caged into the age old regimentations
Why not accept and hold onto them until we're all same?
Why not cut off the prison fences?
Why not let them live like the rest of us?

12. Controlled Conquerors

Men all these days trampled over women
just to hide all the heights they could reach
also the elderly women,
tore the respect of women into shreds
women are demotivated and
made to stay put wherever they are
serving men, and elderly women
Son't you think women are achievers?
I think, and I am one.
Women try to be equal to men,
as they are far superior
and have always beem
The tears women shed are now all saved
No one from far will even be a part
Only us, ourselves have to rise up high
and show how wrong people were.
Just as the volcanoes erupt
Women will stand real and erect.

.

"I think women are foolish to pretend they are equal to men.
They are far superior and always have been. "
- Quoted by Author William Golding.

13. Dilemma

It was the first time I cried,
with eyes dry and heart heavy,
I was into something-
I never once wanted to be.
I, in front of my eyes,
Saw him speaking with another,
I don't know what is was,
Possessiveness, jealousy or whatever.
I wanted him to not be hurt,
aloof me, i was the one hurt
"What is is?" People asked
"Love, what else could it be?"
I was in dilemma,
Should I propose or should I back off?
What do I do? I didnkt know;
Face it! I thought
Love, mine was one-sided,
It did hurt me,
Yet all I did was love him harder,
and hoped it was me at last.

14. Divergence

People with good heart
Are always meant to part
From friends and memories.
Let alone the bad past
Let me carry the good ones.
For the life is tremendously waiting
To let me know that -
"the triumph over it is not an easy joke"

15. Distance

Sometimes, the most hurting thing
Is the most needed one
One such was our distance
You are else were and I am too
But I was never uncertain
I was never doubtful
All I did was loving you,
Loving you with all my heart
Sometimes I feel emptiness within.
Thinking of many reasons
What I got was the distance
And, distance isn't a matter at all
What maters is love
Distance can't make us apart
Maybe death can
just reminding you that I love you
And will always do.

16. For I was in love with you

I was with much of people,
They were all my friends,
Yet I felt so alone,
For I was lost in your thoughts;
You are really special,
And, the reason? I don't know,
Looking through the window glass,
For I was missing you;
Everyone surpassing,
I thought it was you,
Only to smile at my foolishness,
For I was hoping for you;
The school,
I was so excited to come,
And now thinking there wasn't a need,
For I was away from you;
The whole day,
I was thinking about you,
Smiling alone by myself,
For I was in love with you.

17. Friends

Friends are the ones,
who stays till everyends
They are the ones, to-
criticize you, encourage you
At you odds, all the
goods and bads
The understand you,
They stay by your side
Till the end
They are the cute faces
who make you mad
They are the ones
who made you hard,
Enough to face every odds,
The goods and the bads.

18. Haiku

Melody to gloom
wearing away the aching hurt,
I sweep though all the pain.

My life, a misery
a distressing poem it is,
still I live, smiling.

19. Haunting Reality

Reality was scary,
So were my fears,
To let aside all these,
I let slumber slid to me.
Reality was harsh,
So was my dream,
Escapism didn't work,
Cause' reality followed me there
Reality worries me,
So did my expectations,
Daunting and haunting,
But, hurting the most.
Change is human,
But why does it hurt?
May be I pulled you into,
An uncomfortable space,
Away from the 'you',
To what I wanted from you,
Away from reality
To mere expectation
My eyes are dry
And my heart is heavy,

Although it hurts,
All I want is us.

20. Hope

*We don't always trust people
ones we trust don't always stay
in life, trust is a key
to hold any relationship
but the same trust can break us
we always hope for something
it was a hope that we would
surpass this pandemic
but does hope always give positivity?
It doesn't, sometimes we get buried
in the regret of us, hoping
we hope anything that happens
must be good
and trust the ones not to be
broken by heart,
smiling always
I hope, trust never breaks.*

21. Into the depth of my heart

A life imprisonment, my whole life was
Some days it wounded, some days it bled,
But every day was a hurting hell,
Bleeding everywhere,
It pricked and pinched,
Hurting from the very blood
To the water bond.
Every day, through living deaths,
I never stopped weeping inside,
For it was all from my very family,
For it was all from my very friends.
Knives inched deep into the depth of my heart,
Slowly wanting to die the very death,
Floating into the thin air,
Not wanting by anyone,
Or maybe not wanting to be anyone's.
Future's bleak, for it was snatched away,
By boundlessly criticizing and daunting,
By overburdening, leading to self-accusations.
Like the stray dogs' hunger,

Wagging tail over love,
Being faithful for whomsoever,
And then being hit with stones and whatever.
Hurt and bleeding,
I still want to go back,
Wagging tail over love-
This is materialistic for them;
Just to be shooed and again,
Hit with stones and whatever.
Every night, to some drunkard's bark,
I lose my right; to the very domestic slavery.
Once in life, I heard the phrase,
And for lifetime it would ring in my ears –
"You may be a daughter,
But you're a bloody slave."
Blood was stronger- said a proverb,
True – with hatred and hurt;
And not what it actually meant.

22. Lonely me

I feel alone, even when there are
A lot of people around me
Sometimes feeling lonely
Makes me think I am dumb
I am worthless and
Sometime I even consider myself a junk.
I feel alone, even when there are
A lot of people around me
I have wanted a lot of people
I never really experienced reality
I was always in a fantasy
With was really special and memorable.
I feel alone, even when there are
A lot of people around me.

23. Long lonely paths

Long lonely paths, I travelled across
The world now filled with
betraying and backstabbing
Still a part of me lingering in the past
Lonely doesnt really mean
depression or dejection
It just means,
You are better off alone
Sometimes, I love myself
for acceptance of my flaws
Sometimes, I hate myself
for not being loved by any
Long lonely paths, I travelled across
Now, happy and alone.

24. Love

Love was a reason
To surpass our problems
It was a solution
To all the questions aroused
It was a dream for many
It was a nightmare for many
Yet it was a sollution
To all our problems.
We lived together,
the reason love
We lived together,
Just as our love did.

25. Magnificience

Gazing at the blues above,
breeze drifting shreds of hair,
all around so lush and green
Until the end of which is seen.
The burble of the rill afar,
Chirple of the whooper swan,
The dismal of the down pour,
All we do is ignore.
Lush, green and Aqua, clear,
Essence of creation, mother nature.

26. Midnight bloomer

Every night at twelve,
She crept into my mind,
And pushed me into dilemma,
She used every possible way,
To make me smile each new day.
She always said-
I was the best
aI could do anything.
She called me-
"The midnight bloomer".

27. Molestation

Grasses green, temptations high,
Little they are, molestations why?
Infant, teen, adult or grey
One with vagina is always a prey
Seven, eleven, -teen or —ty
Their eyes roam from shoe to tee,
I was ten, with nothing inviting,
Got pulled by the collar into an unfriendly hug
Pushed past the masculine hands,
My eyes weary and watery,
Trusted, were no more trustable,
Fear came when looking at the face now.
I ran and laid between, sister and mother,
"What happened?" mother asked,
To speak up, the words were silence,
"Good night", I said and slept off.
The drunkard, no matter what relation,
No matter how flat or provocative,
A girl is a girl, covered or not,
She is claimed to be inviting.
Next day morning was a nightmare,
Fear of sunrise for the first time,

Fear of facing the same person,
I loved waking up to.
I was young and innocent,
Yet I knew what it was
Years passed, ages grew
Everything changed but never did my fear.
Why suppression over the comfort?
Why oppression over the females?
Hands slid into the skirt,
And said it was short,
The vision roved over the chests,
And said the cleavage showed.
The same lusty eyes,
Roam over burkha or shorts,
The hands, and you know what,
all it wants is pleasure, nothing more or less
Belief of society,
Supress freedom of womenfolk,
Belief of what?
Cause being women for everything.
Why not blame men for tormenting?
Why not teach guys what is and not wrong?

28. Moon and Me

You were a moon and
I was a star amongst millions
It took me years to realize
Even if I was amonst the million
I was me and you were you
Every star had its companion star
I was the only one searching
For the moon amonst the stars
I tried, I captured, I lived
You were on varioud forms
A day full of love, a day a little less
A day a little more less and so on
One fine day you would leave me,
Alone in the dark amongst the other stars
Wanting me to wait for you
You never left me so long
It could be only a night
Every night we would meet
Some eith love, some with fights
Yet we decided not to part
Even when i wait for eternity
It is with hope of you returning

As you would do on every sixteenth
The sky was there, supporting me always
Yet what I wanted was the moon
And never the sky.

29. Quintet of the nature

As you blow, Cedar dances
I have seen you travel different places
How easy it is,
You don't want any visa
You fly as you wish to
You let us breathe
You let us enjoy the moment
You are in every single day of ours
You make my hair wobble as you near me
I cannot see you but I surely can feel your presence.
As you burn, bonfire lits
I have seen you as a bane and a boon
You dazzle among the dark
You heat up the scene
You light up so many lives
You are bright and glistening always
I have always wondered how you always flourish
You bring positivity within
I can see you, feel you,
Your presence creates an optimistic inside.
As you flow, emotions too
I have seen people wait for you

You have always been beautiful
You are the dawn of evolution
Lives originate from you
You are the unfolding of unaswered questions
I have seen you in different forms, all beneficial
You are a remedy for many
You are colourless, yet seen and felt.
As you stay, we live
I have seen you shaky sometimes
But you have always come up great
You don't think of who stamps on you
You live your life for others
Your petrichor when you shower is one of my favorites
You are brown and have deep rooted beings on you
You're brown and yet no racism
If there's no you,
there wouldn't have been us.
As the day dawns, it's so bright up there
You are light and blue
You are afar yet we see you
You are so significant
people try to reach you
You never fall,
You are never felt, but are always seen.

30. She was nowhere

Sometimes I sit alone in the dark,
Thinking, how the world had changed me,
how people changed me,
how she changed me.
It was my fault may be,
But the one who made me,
was her, her sweetness,
her friendliness and her softness.
I was starting to fall for her,
And then, she was nowhere,
Nowhere to be found.
I wanted her to be a bond,
that made me feel secure.
But then I realised that
I could neither be controlled not be loved.
And then she came back,
Just as she left,
made me feel all I wanted,
And then again, she was nowhere.
Sometimes I sit alone in the dark,
Thinking, how the world had changed me,
how people changed me,

how she changed me.

31. Stars

Each time I see you all
the only thing I think is
"You are still together"
I sometimes envy you
Just because I don't have such heart
And I am never able to love like you do
You sparkle if or not people see you
I want to be like you
But i am not able to.

32. The Doom

My heart feels a thousand knives' stabbing,
Over the same wound again and again,
It thudded soundly,
At the thought of, 'how many more?'
If I were a mage,
All I would want is make pain vanish,
The pain of mortality, the pain of death,
The pain of the phrase, 'no more alive'
The wounds are deep,
For which I found no medicine,
Wanting to cry aloud,
Wanting all this to end,
Maybe this is what human life means,
Filled with pain and agony,
With an aching heart I write –
To god, "Let's end this,
At least spare innocent hearts,
Let the world not end,
At least not so soon,
Let me see people smile from heart,
At least before I see my end."
Let alone the pain and past,

Let life be of glee and gaiety.
Some say, "No one starves for too long"
All I ask is —
Why starving when there is a lot more time to?
Why at such an early age?
And why all of a sudden?

33. The Predefined Me

I was me and you were you,
But the difference between were,
You showed your emotion,
While bossing over mine.
Maybe that's because,
You never know 'me',
The real 'me', not because,
I faked myself but because,
I never wanted to break you,
People hid under a mask,
Of happiness, of liveliness,
I hid under a mask, for no reason,
To perfectify me, to accept everything,
For it was easy than to lose someone.
But then I realized, what if,
What if I never showed my devil side?
What if one day it bursts out?
What if the relationship ends?
And, what if there's no more 'us',
I stood alas looking for a reason,
But your ego didn't allow you to give me one,
I cannot always be sweet and sugary,

I am indeed the spicy chilly,
And it took months to come out.

I am an animal sometimes,
An animal you would want to kill,
But, the sweet me is not me,
These are me, not different people,
Just different emotions
Emotions are human,
Emotionless are creatures,
Sweet only isn't me,
I am of mixed of emotions,
I am me not your predefined 'me'.

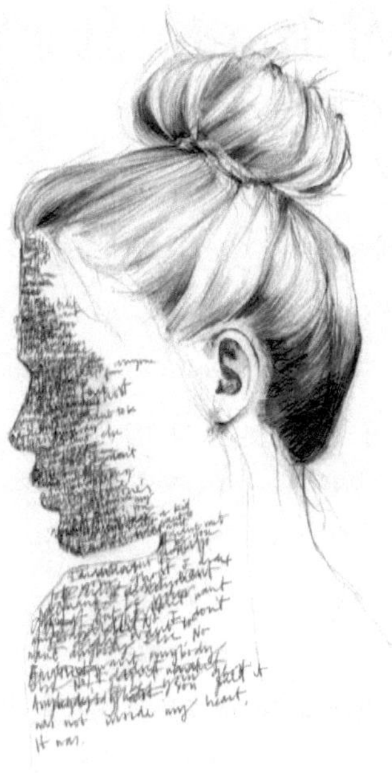

34. With a heavy heart

A little insecurity aroused from within
As you were slowly parting from me
My heart thudded soundly
In the thought of losing you.
A miserable decision of mune
Took you far away from me
Each time I look at you
I feel I had made the biggest mistake.
Letting you alone in your hard times
And expecting you to come back
Is the dumbest thing
I have ever done.
You, were done with me
When I was falling all over again
And now, standing alone
With my little insecurity and a heavy heart.

35. Wreathed onto the reminiscence of you

Love can hurt you,
When hurt is for good,
Love can break you,
When breaking down is for good,
I did get hurt, I did fall,
But it was temporary,
For my love was permanent,
We were not perfect,
We were no matured,
We were we, just like gods in love,
Our imperfections didn't matter,
Reason, our love mattered more,
Misunderstandings and misinterpretations,
Ego for one, and another too,
One knows another pretends not to,
Days were good when it was happy,
Days were terrible when it was not,
Regrets filled, guilty me,
Reason why, ego be
Love is love, Hurt is hurt,

For one was permanent and other was not
Let me be abase, and amiable
For my bowels feels so laden
Perhaps, it was you, the magic,
That made me worship love as god,
My heart is wreathed onto the reminiscence of you
For it was strenuous to give up on you.

36. Womanhood

I was tiny and I didn't know things
A dawn it was, I started bleeding
I was scared to death and screamed loud
My ma came and said, "I mustn't see"
She called her ma and my grandma said,
"Make her stay home; five days!"
And then to me, she said-
You're into women hood,
Stay away from stray dogs,
Don't go near plants and trees,
Don't go into the Pooja place,
Don't sit on the bed,
Don't walk around a lot,
Don't talk to others about this,
Don't smell like a prey,
Don't this and don't that!
I bled for five and I thought
"What if the whole life?"
We bleed for days
And we just don't die
It's regular and irregular
Faces filled with acne

And a lot of hair loss,
And comes the queen of all
Mood swings,
Happy and sad together?
Can you be?
Yes, When you're a girl
And still body shaming,
She's fat, she's thin
She's tall, she's short
"SHE IS SHE"
Why not just accept that.
Pads, Tampons and menstrual cups
Wear and walk around?
Carrying around your tired and aching body
And people ask, "Why are you so lazy?"
Short dresses prohibited
Longs aren't comfortable
Just inside the four walls
Punching out you frustration
Into the same old pillow
And walk out smiling like always
Why is an essential branded as a taboo?
Why not just openly talk
Why not ask men to buy pads when we can't ourselves?
Suffer for life for carrying a baby?
It is indeed womanhood
But why can't others accept the pain

Rather than saying, "It's womanhood"?
I was tiny when I was said —
"You're into the womanhood!"
Eleven, I was —
Just came out of the primary class
What would I know?
May be what people taught me about womanhood,
But later getting to know all those I learnt were
Nothing but nonsense,
What tags along with period is
Cramps, cravings,
Mood swings and mental depression
I wake up in the morning
And find myself on blood stained bed
Instead of patting my shoulder and saying —
"I'll take care, don't worry!"
What my home mates says is —
"Clean it now it looks disgusting!"
"Am I a servant, can't you be aware?"
"How can someone sleep without knowing this?"
"I know how it feels, don't act"
And all I could do is stay mum
And carry the bedspread to wash
The house is heated, Reason?
The so called unsanitary and totally natural process.
And that's a working day too,
I hurry myself and come to the dine

To find, it wasn't prepared yet,
With hungry stomach I leave the house
and reach the school
And there goes the school bell,
You're late! My mind shouts
And then I realise I haven't completed my homework too
My tummy grumbles reminding I hadn't taken my food
And then the cramp follows,
"Ouch!" I say, and the class turns around to me
It's a hell lot of a pain I would say
Not exaggerating, just the truth
Irregular? Take pills
Regular and paining? Take pills
Home remedies, a hot cup of coffee,
But, can we ask for it? It's up to the home mate's mood
I come home and throw my bag and lay on the bed –
"Don't stain the bed, spread a mat"
My back aches, but all they worry about is
Blood Stains on the bed!
I would be scratching my head
To complete the project before deadline
And from nowhere,
"Baby, I'll be with you forever!"
You hear your ex's voice to turn back and find no one
You try to ignore but eventually start crying
And then sadness turns into anger, and then hunger
"Ma! I am hungry!" I shout

And she shouts back to me,
"You don't lift a finger, and you're hungry?"
I crouch on ground and pull up my blankets
And fall asleep without food,
Hourly once your pads start to overflow
Regular changings, and the result is pad rash
After all these adolescence drama,
You step into the actual womanhood,
Parents try to get rid of you in the name of marriage
And then?, "Anything special?"
Becomes a regular talk among the relatives
Infertility? Sterility? Miscarriage? And whatnot?
And then finally pregnancy, nine months and nine days,
The baby evicts itself from the womb,
That's the blessing in disguise I would say
Nine months of bleeding at a stretch?
And still a human being alive?
Yeah, that's a women and that's womanhood.
Homemaker? Or working? Both are indeed working
But working and also a homemaker? That's a mother
Adolescence and adult-hood is over,
And then? Pain is over?
Nope, never, then comes the menopause
Irregular then and irregular now
A months or two skipped and totally stopped
The flow becomes lighter some times and
Much heavier the other

Cancer? Hysterectomy?
And then you smoke too?
The symptoms increases them
And then the causes and symptoms we see,
Insomnia, weight gain, memory problems
Mood changes, Sleep problems and night sweats
Not only these, a lot and lot more
And all you could do is say,
"That's what womanhood is."

37. Yellow woods

Love is yellow woods,
Which comes and never stays,
It's extraordinary,
yet, is ultimately transient.